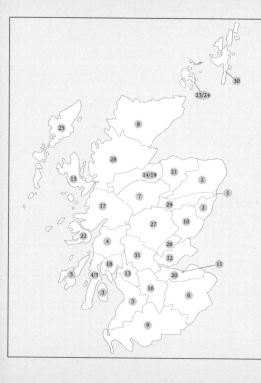

1. Aberdeen
2. Aberdeens⋯⋯⋯⋯⋯⋯⋯ute
3. Arran & A⋯
4. Argyll
5. Southern A⋯
6. The Border⋯
7. The Cairngorms
8. Caithness & Sutherland
9. Dumfries and Galloway
10. Dundee & Angus
11. Edinburgh
12. Fife, Kinross & Clackmannan
13. Glasgow
14. Inverness
15. The Isle of Skye
16. Lanarkshire

23. Orkney
24. Orkney in Wartime
25. The Outer Hebrides
26. The City of Perth
27. Perthshire
28. Ross & Cromarty
29. Royal Deeside
30. Shetland
31. Stirling & The Trossachs

The remaining four books, Caledonia, Distinguished Distilleries, Scotland's Mountains and Scotland's Wildlife feature locations throughout the country so are not included in the above list.

PICTURING SCOTLAND

LOCH LOMOND, COWAL & BUTE

PUTTING GREEN
PAVILION
TENNIS COURTS
PUBLIC LIBRARY
COUNCIL CHAMBERS
BISHOP'S GLEN
TROUT FISHING

WEST BAY	EAST BAY
PUTTING GREENS	POST OFFICE
PADDLING POND	SHOPPING CENTRE
PLAYGROUND	CINEMAS ETC.
BATHING LIDO	BOWLING GREENS
MORAG'S FAIRY GLEN	TENNIS COURTS
BOATING	SPORTS STADIUM
FISHING	GOLF COURSE
BULLWOOD	BOATING & FISHING

COLIN NUTT
Author and photographer

NESS PUBLISHING

2   Ben Lomond seen from Ben Donich, one of the peaks in the southern part of the Arrochar Alps.

LOCH LOMOND, COWAL & BUTE

Welcome to Loch Lomond, Cowal and Bute!

Magical Loch Lomond, with its 'bonnie banks' famed by the well-known traditional song, is where this journey begins. Starting on the western shores of this famous loch we follow the stretch from Luss to Tarbet. This district lies within the Loch Lomond and Trossachs National Park, as does a sizeable part of Cowal. From Loch Lomond we head west up the 'Rest and be Thankful' road to explore the southernmost Arrochar Alps, for these are the peaks that stand at the northern end of the Cowal Peninsula, the region that forms a major part of this journey. From Cowal, the short ferry crossing over the Kyles of Bute brings us to the lovely island which bears that name. The areas covered by this book all lie within the eastern part of the county of Argyll.

Argyll stretches approximately 120 miles up Scotland's western seaboard, incorporates 26 inhabited islands and is a hotbed of ancient history. The magnificent realm of land and water, with its many sea lochs and islands, make Argyll's coastline longer than that of France; its landmass of 6,930 sq. km. makes it larger than Belgium. The name 'Argyll' comes from the Gaelic *Earra-Ghaidheal* meaning the boundary of the Gaels. It was indeed frontier territory, for the Gaels, a people of Celtic ethnicity who migrated from Ireland, inevitably found other peoples already established. Nevertheless, by about 500AD they were able to establish the kingdom of Dál Riata

Helensburgh's Central (terminus) station is quite grand, still in possession of its original canopies, 5
and attractively maintained – note the floral displays on the platform.

in what we now call Argyll. This is such a large part of Scotland that two further volumes in this series are required to cover the rest of it (see the front endpaper for a list of the other titles available).

Although part of the Scottish mainland, the Cowal Peninsula has something of an island 'feel' to it, not least because much of it is more easily accessed by water than by road. It has never been on the railway map. Dunoon, with a population of about 8,300, is one of Argyll's two largest towns (Oban being the other). Access to it from the rest of the mainland is much more practical – and enjoyable – by ferry from Gourock, a route that supports two services, than by a very circuitous road journey. The short sea crossing was a big part of its appeal – an adventure, even – leading to its growth back in the 19th century when wealthy Glasgow businessmen built their holiday homes here. And when 'paid holidays' were introduced, the masses flocked 'doon the watter' to enjoy the many recreational activities laid on for them.

The stunning little Isle of Bute grew under the same influences as it too is within easy travelling distance from Clydeside. Given its modest size – approximately 15 miles long and four miles wide you could, if you wish, take a holiday from motoring and leave the car behind! By far the best way to engage with this island is to take the train to Wemyss Bay and walk straight on to the ferry. Once on Bute, excellent bus services will transport you around the island.

Firstly though, on the way to Loch Lomond, we need to take in the town of Helensburgh as it is nowadays part of Argyll, having formerly belonged to Dunbartonshire. Despite being a relatively recent addition to Argyll, it is a good place to set the tone and establish the mood for an exploration of its eastern districts. Turn the pages and enjoy the trip!

As well as the obvious attraction of the seafront, Helensburgh's beautifully presented gardens, such as here at Hermitage Park, provide a relaxing environment in which to unwind.

8   Loch Lomond and its larger islands as seen from the hills on its western side. By area, this is Britain's largest inland loch, covering some 71,000,000m² (that's 27.5 square miles), with an

average depth of 37m/121ft. Its greatest depth however is 190m/623ft. The loch contains a staggering 2,600,000,000m³ of water!

10 When visiting Helensburgh, a visit to Hill House is a must! Regarded as Charles Rennie Mackintosh's finest domestic architecture, Mackintosh and his wife Margaret also designed all the interior fittings.

Left: part of the gardens at Hill House. Right: Colquhoun Square in Helensburgh. The planned town **11** we see today was the creation of Sir Ian Colquhoun and named after his wife, Helen.

12 A superb display of colour at Geilston Garden, a few miles from Helensburgh near Cardross. Developed over 200 years ago, it is a testimony to landscape design.

Equally colourful, these hanging baskets and window boxes adorn a cottage in the village of Luss on the shores of Loch Lomond. This is a delightful setting, just a minute or so from … 13

14 ... the lochside beach at Luss. The boat on the right is one of several that offer trips around Loch Lomond, enabling a better view of the wildlife or a chance to explore the islands.

For a more energetic form of exercise, the walk up Beinn Dubh, the hill that rises above Luss, is **15** most rewarding, even if only the lower summit is achieved, seen just right of centre.

16 From this elevation, a wonderful Loch Lomond panorama opens up, showing just what a complex pattern of islands occupies this part of the loch. There are 37 islands in all.

A closer look down on Luss. A settlement has probably existed here since the 1300s, when it is **17** known that there was a church dedicated to St Kessog, who lived on a nearby island 700 years earlier.

18 About eight miles north up Loch Lomond we come to Tarbet, one of the main embarkation points for loch cruises. The summit of Ben Lomond (974m/3195ft) can just be seen.

Loch Lomond is much narrower here, hemmed in by the surrounding hills. One of the cruise **19** destinations reached from Tarbet is Inversnaid on the opposite side of the loch.

20 It's easy to pass Tarbet by when concentrating on choosing the right road (it is the junction of the A82 and A83), but it's preferable to linger a while and soak up the scenery.

Hillwalking in this area is not too demanding but offers some great and less familiar views. **21**
For example, here is an unusual 'take' on The Cobbler (884m/2900ft).

22 Seen from the slopes of Beinn Dubh, the northern reaches of Loch Lomond and the surrounding craggy hills paint an archetypal picture of Scottish scenery.

There are several Munros (Scottish hills over 914m/3000ft) in the Arrochar Alps, one of which is **23** distant Beinn Narnain, topping out at 926m/3038ft.

24 One of Scotland's great views: Ben Lomond towers above the loch and in the distance on the left are enough further mountains to keep even the most enthusiastic hill walkers occupied for a long time!

Ben Lomond is usually climbed from Rowardennan, visible to the right of the picture on the far side **25** of the loch. Part of the path can just be made out on the hillside.

26 Moving west to the Cowal Peninsula, the mountains of which are here reflected in Loch Fyne. Beinn an Lochain (901m/2956ft) with its dramatic overhang can just be seen at top right.

Ben Donich will provide us with a perfect platform from its 847m/2779ft summit to survey
the surrounding territory.

28 Despite not looking very snowy from lower down, when the higher levels are reached another world is encountered. On the right is Beinn an Lochain, looking somewhat formidable.

Windblown snow sculptures add an artistic touch near the top of Ben Donich. The bright peak **29** in the distance is Ben Lomond.

30 Looking down from way up high at the inner end of Loch Goil (a branch of Loch Long) and Lochgoilhead which was much more accessible in the days when a regular steamer service operated.

The village of Lochgoilhead grew up in the 19th century thanks to that service. In the season of **31** 'mists and mellow fruitfulness' it is tinged with the pinkish light of low sun through the mist.

32 In brighter conditions up above, this gives an idea of the rugged nature of the surrounding mountain tops and a distant horizon of even higher peaks many miles away.

Expeditions on short winter days provide plenty of low-sun images. The mountain tops are lonely places in these conditions. The photographer's bag and walking pole add some scale to the scene.

34 Ardkinglas Woodland Garden is situated below these mountains on the shores of Loch Fyne. There are several lovely walks throughout the gardens that yield scenes like this.

Ardkinglas House was completed in the autumn of 1907 after a construction period of only eighteen **35** months. Public tours are available from April to October on the last Friday of every month.

36 Magnificent trees at Ardkinglas: left, this massive silver fir has been designated one of the 50 Great British Trees. Right: the tallest tree in Britain, which measures 64m/210ft.

Travelling south from Ardkinglas, this is Loch Eck in the Argyll Forest Park. When mist restricts the **37** view, it is perhaps easier to notice some of the finer details that catch the eye on a day like this.

38 Loch Long is well named, a finger of sea that reaches about 15 miles inland, right up to Arrochar. The buildings across the water are at the Royal Naval Armaments Depot at Coulport.

The Church of St Munn was founded beside Holy Loch in the 10th century. On the left is the ruin of the tower of the 1442-built church. The present church dates from 1841.

40 St Munn's Church and the village of Kilmun sit on the north shore of Holy Loch, seen here at sunset with the Cowal hills rising beyond the waters.

We now head north for a few miles to the 120-acre Benmore Botanic Garden which boasts over 300 species of rhododendron. Here we see the Dolphin Pond.

42 A riot of autumn colour surrounds another of Benmore's ponds. Benmore is one of three regional gardens belonging to The Royal Botanic Garden Edinburgh.

Left: perhaps the most spectacular sight at Benmore is the avenue of Giant Redwoods. **43**
Right: in Dunoon, the statue of 'Highland Mary', who was once betrothed to Robert Burns.

44 The resort town of Dunoon stands on the east coast of the Cowal Peninsula overlooking the Clyde estuary. This view looks across Castle Gardens to Queen's Hall.

From Castle Gardens, the Clyde estuary stretches away towards Glasgow. The distinctive ferry **45** terminal is in the middle distance, from which the main route crosses over to Gourock.

46 From the ferry we see the other side of the terminal with Castle House behind. Castle House was built 1822-4 by James Ewing, Lord Provost of Glasgow, and today houses the town's museum.

Lingering afterglow over Dunoon's West Bay. Dunoon is an excellent centre from which to explore **47** the area and offers visitors a great variety of recreational pursuits – see the signpost on p.1!

48 Southwards from Dunoon leads to Toward. In 1821 a former Lord Provost of Glasgow, Kirkman Finlay, built Castle Toward, seen here from the Isle of Bute ferry.

Moving over to the western side of Cowal, this is Kilmodan Church in Glendaruel. A group of **49** carved grave slabs is exhibited in a burial aisle within the churchyard.

50 South from Glendaruel we reach the village of Tighnabruaich, a Gaelic name meaning 'the house on the hill'; many houses do indeed cling to the steep hillsides here.

Tighnabruaich faces the Kyles of Bute, the stretches of sea that surround the northern part of the **51** Isle of Bute. This is the western side of the Kyles, looking south …

52 … and here is the eastern side, with Bute on the right. The road that navigates this area has been described as 'the best scenic drive in Scotland' – hardly an exaggeration on a day like this.

With appetite whetted by the previous scenes, now it's time to discover the Isle of Bute itself. 53
This aerial view of Rothesay, its capital, includes the paddle steamer *Waverley*, upper left.

54 When arriving by ferry this is the first view of Rothesay. Since Victorian times millions of holiday-makers have made the voyage 'doon the watter' from the Glasgow area.

Rothesay is a wonderfully colourful place! Its gardens, such as these on the promenade, **55** are superbly presented and provide a great place from which to watch the world go by.

56 This view from the hillside above the town centre looks towards the ferry terminal. This area was built on reclaimed land, the original shoreline being about 200m inland. By the late 1800s, the

number of steamers calling at Rothesay had increased to the point where its steamer pier was the second busiest on the Clyde.

58 More of the esplanade gardens. This elaborate fountain backed by palm trees and hydrangeas has a distinctly exotic look to it.

Bute is close enough to the mainland to offer fine views in its direction. The hills in the distance **59** are above Toward, the area pictured back on p.48.

60 Left: Rothesay War Memorial. Right: the marina within the harbour. The long, low, green structure is the old cabbie's stand, where carriages used to meet the ferries.

From inside the cab stand, the more commercial side of the harbour is seen, from which **61** a number of fishing boats still operate.

62 Now we turn our attention to Rothesay Castle. Turn back to p.53 for a bird's-eye view.
Above left: looking through the walls to the town. Right: the gatehouse and moat.

The castle interior. Its circular curtain wall makes it unique among Scottish castles. It has stood here **63** since the early 1200s, at which time it fronted on to the bay, before the days of land reclamation.

64 Looking across Rothesay Bay from the east as the ferry docks. Caledonian MacBrayne's vessels take 35 minutes to cross to Wemyss Bay on the mainland.

Beyond the queue of cars waiting to board the ferry are the Winter Gardens, built between the **65** two World Wars, which now form the excellent Isle of Bute Discovery Centre.

66 The steep hillsides rising up from the town centre have caused the construction of this zigzag road known at The Serpentine, a distinctive feature of Rothesay.

A few miles south of Rothesay is Mount Stuart, Britain's most astounding Victorian gothic mansion. **67**
It is home to the Stuarts of Bute, descendants of the Royal House of Stuart.

68   Mount Stuart's truly stunning Marble Hall combines the spirit of Arthurian legend with the luxurious palaces of Greece, Rome and Byzantium and the great Cathedrals of medieval Europe.

The flamboyant house and its 300 acres of gardens reflect the artistic, religious and astrological **69** interests of the 3rd Marquess of Bute. As this view shows, it overlooks the Clyde estuary.

70 A magnificent display of hydrangeas at Mount Stuart. The gardens were designed upon an exquisite natural canvas provided by the island's lush habitat and picturesque shoreline.

Now venturing north of Rothesay, Kames Castle is a lovely, privately owned estate and family home
situated by Kames Bay. The keep seen here was built in the 1300s.

72 Port Bannatyne, formerly known as Kamesburgh, is situated about a mile-and-a-half north of Rothesay and offers a quieter alternative for those seeking views like this. It used to be connected to

Rothesay by electric tram, which continued across the island to Ettrick Bay; the pier harks back to the times when steamers called here. The Cowal hills are in the distance.

74 Port Bannatyne's 100-berth marina opened in 2009, an appropriate development as boat building used to be an industry here.

A final foray to the south of Bute and arrival at Kilchattan Bay reveals a beach and village of the
same name. At low tide the beach is clearly a rich feeding ground for these oystercatchers.

76 Across on the west side of this part of Bute, the Bronze Age standing stones at Kingarth can be located just off the minor road that goes to St Blane's Chapel.

Continue south along this road and the Iron Age hill fort of Dunagoil comes into view on a commanding headland, with the rugged mountains of Arran providing a dramatic backdrop.

78 We end this journey at the end of the road to the southern tip of Bute from where a short walk brings us to the remains of St Blane's Church, some aspects of which are pictured here.